For my very belo[...]
the Em-Fis[...]

SEAGROVE
POTTERIES
THROUGH TIME

STEPHEN C. COMPTON

AMERICA
THROUGH TIME®
ADDING COLOR TO AMERICAN HISTORY

To Polly, the Pottery Lady

AMERICA THROUGH TIME® is an imprint of Fonthill Media LLC

First published 2013, reprinted 2016

Copyright © Stephen C. Compton 2013, 2016

ISBN 978-1-62545-007-4

Typeset in Mrs Eaves XL Serif Narrow
Printed and bound in England

Connect with us:
 www.twitter.com/USAthroughtime
 www.facebook.com/AmericaThroughTime

Sales and Distribution by Arcadia Publishing:
Telephone: 843-853-2070
Fax: 843-853-0044
E-mail: sales@arcadiapublishing.com
For customer service and orders:
Toll-Free 1-888-313-2665

AMERICA THROUGH TIME® is a registered trademark of Fonthill Media LLC

INTRODUCTION

Near the very center of North Carolina lies a village called Seagrove, known far and wide as the *Pottery Town*. The road from Seagrove to the town of Robbins is officially designated the *Pottery Highway*. It's not the only place where pottery has been made in North Carolina, but when you say *Seagrove* to people who know the place, they know that you are probably talking about pottery.

To those who take pleasure in owning old and new North Carolina pottery, the name Seagrove is more the moniker of an ideal than it is of one place. It's true that many potters today are located within and very near the town's boundaries. But the potteries most associated with Seagrove through time have also been located beyond its borders in as many as six neighboring counties.

Utilitarian pottery was first made in the Seagrove area long before the town was chartered in 1913. In fact, Quaker potters from Pennsylvania and Nantucket Island brought their craft to the region as long ago as the 1750s. Since then, there's never been a time when potters didn't turn out wares there for household and decorative use. Today, within a few miles of Seagrove, in what is one of the largest concentrations of potters anywhere in the nation, hundreds of artisans create beautifully turned and brightly glazed wares satisfying the desires of customers from all over the country.

The region's first potters made useful churns, crocks, jugs, and other vessels required for everyday use. They made earthenware, sometimes called redware, and salt-glazed stoneware in long, arched, wood-fired furnaces called groundhog kilns, and in small updraft kilns. Some of the pottery was hauled for sale in covered wagons to outlying places, while some of it was purchased directly from the potters. A Randolph County letter writer in 1876 tells her niece that during her visit to Evan Cole's pottery shop, "Rossinah got a stone churn and milk pans and pie dishes and saw a teapot but did not buy that. I got you a cake mole with blue decorate since you admired mine so long. Hope you do like it well." At the time, members of the Cole family had been making pottery nearby for at least one or two more generations. Cole family potters continue to work at the trade today.

Declining demand for utilitarian pottery in the waning years of the nineteenth-century and early years of the twentieth-century led to the demise of many old shops. A few old-line potters successfully transitioned their craft from the production of utilitarian wares to the creation of decorative art pottery. Raleigh socialites Jacques and Juliana Busbee are credited with the establishment of Moore County's Jugtown Pottery, using their artistic and marketing sensibilities combined with the skills of local area potters to create the area's first successful art pottery shop by the year 1921. Following closely in their footsteps were Jason Cole, who created J. B. Cole's Pottery just a stone's throw from Seagrove, about 1922, and Henry and Rebecca Palmer Cooper who started North State Pottery in Lee County, about 1924. Other successful art pottery shops in the region included Auman Pottery, C. C. Cole Pottery, Carolina Pottery, M. L. Owens Pottery, North State Pottery, Rainbow Pottery (later A. R. Cole Pottery), Royal Crown Pottery and Porcelain Co., Smithfield Art Pottery, and Teague Pottery. Although some of these shops, and others like them not named here, were located in nearby counties some distance away from Seagrove, all employed potters who learned the trade close to Seagrove.

Never large-scale factories like some in the northeastern or midwestern U. S., or like the Staffordshire potteries in England, these were small to mid-sized operations run by farmer-potters who employed relatives, neighbors, and an occasional journeyman potter or two. These shops' output, quality, and longevity were remarkable.

Some of the region's contemporary potters are direct descendents of the original potters who established their shops, or worked for others, in Seagrove area communities bearing colorful names like Whynot, Black Ankle, Steeds, Hemp, Spies, Michfield, and Erect. Some of them have learned through apprenticeships with master potters and others have been university trained at places like Alfred University.

Annually, thousands of visitors come to the Seagrove area where they purchase tens of thousands of pieces of pottery. The North Carolina Pottery Center is a good place to begin when visiting the Seagrove potteries. Conveniently located in the small downtown district, this museum and educational center was opened in 1998 as an outgrowth of a private museum once operated by potters Dorothy and Walter Auman. NCPC's mission is to promote public awareness of North Carolina's remarkable pottery heritage. In addition to its permanent and changing exhibits, examples of the region's contemporary potters' work is displayed and maps are provided to guide visitors to the area's more than one hundred potteries.

OLD POTTERY FAMILIES ACTIVE TODAY: Family names associated with the Seagrove area's first potteries, like Craven, Cole, Chrisco, Luck, McNeill, Owen, and Teague, are familiar to today's pottery customers since members of all of these families continue to work in the trade today. Owens Pottery's claim to be the oldest North Carolina pottery is based upon its early entry into the art pottery trade, following a long family history of utilitarian pottery production. Its founder, James H. Owen (1866-1923), made some of the first wares for Jugtown Pottery.

CRAVENS AMONG STATE'S FIRST POTTERS: Originally from New Jersey, and later, Augusta County, Virginia, members of the Peter Craven (*c.* 1712-1793) family were among the first potters to settle in eighteenth-century North Carolina. Thomas Craven (1742-1817), a son of Peter Craven, was the progenitor of a long line of potters. Thomas Craven's grave is located in a Coleridge (Randolph County, NC) cemetery. His great-grandson, John Anderson Craven (1824-1858), made this salt-glazed stoneware jug, bearing ash runs and his initials, J.A.C.

QUAKER POTTERS BROUGHT CRAFT
TO REGION: Families affiliated with
the Society of Friends (Quakers) came to
the Seagrove region as early as the 1750s,
beginning their journeys in Pennsylvania,
and Nantucket Island. They brought with
them highly developed skills required for
making plain and decorated earthenware.
Members of the Hockett family were among
the region's first Quaker potters, including
William Hockett III (1799-1880) and Himelius
Mendenhall Hockett (1825-1913), seen here.
Photos courtesy of Jane Coltraine Norwood.

NORTH CAROLINA POTTERY CENTER: The North Carolina Pottery Center, a museum and educational center opened in 1998, is a good place to begin exploring Seagrove's many potteries. Located near the center of Seagrove, NCPC hosts a permanent collection of historic and contemporary pottery, and is the site for changing pottery exhibits throughout the year. Examples of pottery made in nearby shops are displayed, and maps are provided, aiding visitors in their search for shops to visit and pottery to buy. *Photos courtesy of North Carolina Pottery Center.*

A VILLAGE DEVOTED TO POTTERY: Standing near the center of the downtown district, a visitor cannot miss the fact that everywhere you turn there is evidence that Seagrove is a pottery town! In addition to the North Carolina Pottery Center, the town hosts the Museum of North Carolina Traditional Pottery, and is the site of annual pottery festivals, including the Celebration of Seagrove Potters, and Seagrove Pottery Festival, both conducted each year on the weekend before Thanksgiving.

COLE NAME SYNONYMOUS WITH POTTERY-MAKING: Raphard Cole (1799-1862) and his son, Evan Cole (1834-1895), were early Cole potters. "Raph" was the son of Mark, and grandson of hatter Stephen Cole (b. 1734), originally from Chester, Pennsylvania, who moved to a site near Seagrove in the 1770s. At least two dozen of Evan's descendents made pottery. Historic Cole art pottery shops include J. B. Cole's Pottery, A. R. Cole Pottery, C. C. Cole Pottery, Carolina Craft Pottery, Clarence Cole Pottery and Smithfield Art Pottery. *Photos courtesy of Charles G. Zug III.*

Decorated Earthenware Some of First Made: Though known for their plain style, Quaker potters decorated some earthenware with oxide-tinted slips. Quaker William Dennis (1769-1847), whose pottery was located near New Salem in northern Randolph County, probably produced this large dish. Much of its decoration is now worn away by generations of use. The marbled teapot and striped dish below were found in Randolph County. The dish on the right is attributed to Solomon Loy, who worked in an area that is Alamance County today.

POTTERY FAR AND NEAR:
With about one hundred potters at work today in scattered, rural locations around Seagrove, the opportunities to buy pottery during a visit to the area are numerous. For the less venturesome type, shops like Seagrove Pottery, seen here, sell the wares of many potters, all in one location. Nearby, restaurants, like Jugtown Café, cater to hungry, and perhaps pottery-quest weary visitors.

IF AT FIRST YOU DON'T SUCCEED...

If one shop or gallery fails to satisfy, another is just a brief walk away in Seagrove's downtown district. Just steps away from numerous working pottery shops and two museum sites, multi-dealer galleries, like the Co-Op of Seagrove Potters, and Village Pottery, provide visitors with a choice of wares for purchase. One of the newest Seagrove pottery shops, Seagrove Creations Pottery Gallery, opened in 2007, and is located just a brief drive away from the town center.

PRESENT INFORMED BY
ANCIENT TRADITION: Seagrove
is no made-up place, created like a
manufacturers' outlet mall for the
purpose of promoting commerce.
Its heritage as a pottery-making
community is deeply rooted in
the work of potters like Daniel
Zebedee Craven (1873-1949), seen
here standing in front of his Moore
County pottery, and potter and
postmaster, William Davis (b. 1847),
the grandfather of Rock House
Pottery's Carolyn Poole. *Craven
Pottery photo courtesy of The State
Archives of North Carolina. Davis image
courtesy of Carolyn Kennedy Poole.*

FROM SEAGROVE TO SMITHSONIAN: William Henry Chrisco (1857-1944) stands in front of his log pottery shop. The entire shop was later dismantled and moved to the Smithsonian Institution. This iconic photo shows pottery crocks lined up to catch rainwater for shop use, a clay storage bin, and a pug mill used for grinding and mixing clay. In addition to stoneware, Chrisco probably produced some earthenware pottery, like the much-cherished "dirt dishes" seen stacked here, used for baking breads and pies. *W. H. Chrisco photo courtesy of Chris Luther.*

POTTERIES IN EVERY NOOK AND CRANNY: A day can be spent in the tiny town center of Seagrove visiting museums, potteries, and galleries. But a quick drive out of town past Pottery Junction takes visitors to dozens of potteries found along winding country roads, some with names like Auman Clay Pond, and Potter's Way. If pottery is not your thing, the North Carolina Zoological Park is a few miles away, and nearby Uwharrie National Forest lands offer many opportunities for outdoor activity.

FORGET YOUR MAP? FOLLOW THE
SIGNS: No need to worry if you fail to
pick up a map showing pottery locations
during your visit to Seagrove. Just keep
your car moving in almost any direction
away from town, and signs will direct
you to nearby potteries. Here, signs
mounted at the intersection of Old
US Highway 220 and Cagle Road tout
the location of four potteries, while
markers posted on an advantageously
located tree on highway 705, the 'Pottery
Highway', make it clear that many
potteries are close by.

OLD IMAGES SHOW PAST WAYS:
An old photograph of a family's
pottering relative is as important as
a jug or jar marked with their name.
Sid Luck, of Luck's Ware Pottery, who
is related to both the Luck and Cole
pottery families, prizes these photos
of brothers, Addison Elbert "Adelbert"
(1890-1952) and Emerson "Bud" Luck
(1886-1951), who were sons of potter
William Henry Luck (1846-1918). Ad
Luck centers a ball of clay on his wheel,
while Bud Luck brings big salt-glazed
jars from his log shop. *Photos courtesy of
Sid Luck.*

FOLLOW THE ROAD OR LOOK FOR
SMOKE: In 2002, the NC Department
of Transportation dubbed highway 705,
the 'Pottery Highway'. Many potteries can
be found on this route, along its scenic
pathway between the towns of Seagrove
and Robbins. Most potters sell their wares
on site, while some only sell during special
"kiln opening" events. Occasionally, a
fortunate visitor arrives at a pottery just
when a potter is burning a load of wares in
a wood-fired kiln, an amazing conflagration
of fire and clay to behold. *Kiln photo courtesy
of Ben Owen III.*

OLD POTTERS CAN LEARN NEW TRICKS: When ready access to glass and metal containers reduced the demand for utilitarian pottery, many potters left the trade for farming or factory work. A few, like potter James H. Owen, successfully adapted his knowledge of materials and technology to produce wares intended more for home decoration than for utility. Here, Jim Owen prepares clay, while his wife, Martha Jane Scott Owen (1874-1953), hand sculpts salt shakers shaped like chickens. *Photos courtesy of the North Carolina Folklife Institute.*

EVOLUTION REQUIRES ADAPTATION:
Old-line potters who failed to transform their old ways into new wares faded away from the trade, while others, like J. H. Owen, found ways to survive. Owen made decorative vases like these using familiar clay, glaze materials, colorful oxides, and his traditional wood-fired groundhog kiln. Except for form, and a dash of added incised and cobalt-painted decoration, Owen's examples are indistinct as a product from the lidded canning jar, seen here, made by a relative, James J. Owen (1830-1905).

AVERY POTTERY AND TILEWORKS: First trained in the 1990s as an apprentice to Sid Oakley at Cedar Creek Gallery in Creedmoor, North Carolina, Blaine Avery later studied glaze formulation with Lanna Wilson and Pete Pennel at Gatlinburg's Arrowmont School of Crafts. He opened his Seagrove shop and gallery in 2002. This set of peacock vases is made of wheel thrown, salt-glazed stoneware decorated with slip colored porcelain beneath a translucent copper glaze. This technique is a feature of Blaine's pottery. *Photos courtesy of Blaine Avery.*

BEN OWEN POTTERY: Ben Owen III continues a family tradition traced back many generations. Ben's grandfather, and namesake, was the master potter for Jugtown Pottery before opening Old Plank Road Pottery, in 1959. Ben was mentored by his grandfather before studying ceramics at East Carolina University, and then Japan. His work reflects traditional North Carolina designs and techniques, as well as oriental translations. Ben's more monumental works are found in public and private settings alike. *Photos courtesy of Ben Owen III.*

A TRADITION HANDED DOWN:
Intermarriage among North Carolina's
pottering families was commonplace.
Potter Rufus Owen (1872-1948), seen
here, married Martha McNeill, the
daughter of potter Malcolm McNeill (b.
c. 1845). Their three sons, Charlie, Ben,
and Joe Owen were potters, as was Ben's
son, Wade, and grandson, Ben Owen III.
Similarly, two sons and a grandson of
Paschal McCoy (1816-1876), who made
this salt-glazed stoneware jar, were
potters. *Rufus and Martha Owen photo
courtesy of Ben Owen III.*

SALT-GLAZED STONEWARE A
POTTERY MAINSTAY: Seagrove area
potters excelled at the production of
salt-glazed stoneware. One of the finest
stoneware makers in the region was
Chester Webster (1799-1882), a potter
who learned the trade in Hartford,
Connecticut, before coming to North
Carolina in the early 1800s. He made
this one-gallon jug featuring a finely
incised image of a bird on its side.
Other superb nineteenth-century
turners in the region were Nicholas
(1797-1858) and Himer Jacob Fox (1826-
1909), of Chatham County, who made
the two jugs seen here.

BULLDOG POTTERY: Named for their bulldogs, Moka and Babu, Bulldog Pottery was established by Bruce Gholson and Samantha Henneke in 2000. Their products are an eclectic mix of form, imagery, texture, and pattern. Bruce received a BFA degree from the University of Georgia, and a MFA from Alfred University. Samantha also holds a BFA from Alfred University. A mastery of form and glaze is evident in the collection of Bulldog Pottery wares seen here. *Photos courtesy of Bruce Gholson and Samantha Henneke.*

CADY CLAY WORKS: John Mellage, of Cady Clay Works, stokes the firebox of his Japanese-styled anagama kiln, the first of its kind built in the Seagrove community. When fired, it takes a month of pot-making to fill, three days to load, and fifty-five hours of non-stop wood-burning to achieve a blistering 2,400° F. John focuses on wheel thrown production while his wife, co-owner Beth Gore, majors in the creation of hand-built pieces. *Photos courtesy of John Mellage and Beth Gore.*

GRAVE MARKERS AMONG RAREST FORMS: Grave markers made of salt-glazed stoneware rank among the most unusual objects ever made by Seagrove area potters. The markers seen here in a cemetery are associated with the Teague family, and the solo marker was made for Demsey Cagle, a Confederate veteran who died in 1883. It is likely that potters from the Teague and Cagle families made these markers for family members. *Cemetery photo courtesy of The State Archives of North Carolina.*

TRANSITIONS FROM PAST TO PRESENT: A century ago, a move from utilitarian pottery forms to the creation of decorative wares depended upon the knowledge and experience of old-line Seagrove area potters. This early Jugtown Pottery example may be the product of one of its first on-site potters, Charles G. "Charlie" Teague (1901-1938). Early in form and materials, colorful splashes of slip added an artsy look. *Charlie Teague photo courtesy of North Carolina Collection, University of North Carolina at Chapel Hill Library. Bayard Wootten photo.*

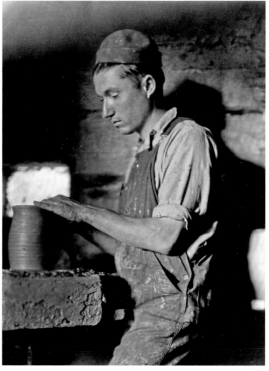

CHAD BROWN POTTERY: Chad Brown's grandfather was potter Graham Chriscoe (1928-2012), and his great-grandfather was Henry (W. H.) Chrisco (1857-1944), a traditional potter whose salt-glazed wares command high prices today. Long a journeyman working for other potters, Chad now operates his own shop. While construction of his own kiln is under way, he often uses the North Carolina Pottery Center's groundhog kiln. Chad can often be found demonstrating pottery-making for NCPC visitors. *Photos courtesy of Chad Brown.*

CHRIS LUTHER POTTERY: With his family heritage linked to his great-grandfather, Henry (W. H.) Chrisco, and as many as four other Chrisco family potters, Chris Luther's pedigree as a potter runs deep. Here, Chris is seen "capping" a big jar, a process whereby two or more separately turned sections are joined together to create pots too large to be turned in one piece. The vase seen here displays a beautiful Shino glaze. *Photos courtesy of Chris Luther.*

BEN OWEN GENERATES JUGTOWN
SUCCESS: Early images of Benjamin
Wade Owen Sr. (1904-1983) show him
creating handmade wares that made
Busbee-owned Jugtown Pottery famous.
Many of the first products produced by
him for Jugtown Pottery were sold in a
Greenwich Village, New York shop called
The Village Store, a business purchased by
North Carolinian Juliana Busbee from Alice
Palmer around 1917. *Bayard Wootten photos
courtesy of North Carolina Collection, University
of North Carolina at Chapel Hill Library.*

JUGTOWN GROUNDED IN CRAFT MOVEMENT: Jacques (1870-1947) and Juliana (1877-1962) Busbee's Jugtown Pottery built its success on the nation's interest in things handmade when industrialization was leaving its mark on nearly everything "made in America." Here, Juliana sits in her Jugtown cabin home, surrounded by handcrafted pottery and pewter. In 1952, Jugtown weaver, Guy Weatherly Jr. (1925-1965), sits at a loom with a traditional woven coverlet hanging nearby. *Photos courtesy of The State Archives of North Carolina. Weatherly photo by Albert Barden.*

COLE'S POTTERY: Though located near Sanford, in Lee County, no shop has deeper Seagrove roots than Cole's Pottery, first established by Arthur Ray Cole (1892-1974), whose family made pottery in Randolph County for many generations. Cole's daughter, Neolia (1927-), who is the current owner of Cole's Pottery, glazes pottery as she has done for more than eight decades. These examples were made by her. Sisters Celia (1925-), and Neolia Cole were the 2003 recipients of the North Carolina Folk Heritage Award.

CRYSTAL KING POTTERY: Best known for her folk art figures, Crystal King is the daughter of Seagrove area potters, Terry and Anna King, of King's Pottery. At age seven, Crystal made her first clay figure at the site of the old Seagrove Pottery operated by the late Dorothy and Walter Auman. Many of her creations, like her popular Noah's Arks, which come complete with a menagerie of animals, reflect biblical themes. *Photos courtesy of Crystal King.*

Many Hands Make Beautiful Craft: Images from Jugtown Pottery's early years of operation demonstrate how more than a potter's work alone is required to create saleable objects of beauty. Here, with a mule's help, Ernest Williamson (1903-1971) grinds clay in a rustic pug mill before Rancie Moore (1903-1962) makes it into "balls," like the one seen here, for turning by potter Ben Owen Sr. *Photos courtesy of The State Archives of North Carolina. Bill Sharpe photos.*

THE WORK IS ENDLESS: Once turned by the potter, air dried, and sometimes bisque-fired to harden the clay, wares are glazed in preparation for a final burning in a wood-fired groundhog kiln. In 1938, Jugtown workers Ernest Williamson and Rancie Moore coat objects with glaze before loading them into the kiln. Each successful burning of a kiln full of wares requires many hours of arduous labor, and many cords of wood. *Photos courtesy of The State Archives of North Carolina. Bill Sharpe photos.*

DANIEL JOHNSTON POTTERY:
For four years an apprentice of potter
Mark Hewitt, Daniel Johnston also
studied with England's Clive Bowen,
and Thailand's Sawein Silakhom. In
2010, his ambitious *Large Jar Project*
created one hundred wood-fired pots,
each one made from one hundred
pounds of clay. When offered for
sale, anxious buyers snapped up all
one hundred jars in twenty minutes.
Daniel uses local clays and his glaze
is concocted with ash from his wood
stove. *Photos courtesy of Daniel Johnston.*

DEAN AND MARTIN POTTERY: Jeffrey Dean began his pottery career in the 1990s following the completion of a BFA in ceramics from East Carolina University. Stephanie Martin earned a BFA in design from UNC at Greensboro. Her output includes coil-built, slab-built, and sculptural work like this triptych extolling the Women's Liberation Movement. She describes her work as "an exploration of recollections of the past, and our ability to use these experiences to define and shape our personalities." *Photos courtesy of Jeffrey Dean and Stephanie Martin.*

JUGTOWN ENDURES TWISTS AND TURNS: In 1959, Jugtown Pottery closed due to litigation surrounding the affairs of an aging Juliana Busbee. After thirty-seven years as its potter, Ben Owen quit Jugtown Pottery. John Maré (1914-1962), whose friend Al Powers made this sculpted horse, was made general manager of the pottery when it reopened. Following Maré's death, the pottery was acquired by Country Roads, Inc., a non-profit led by Nancy Sweezy (1921-2010). Vernon Owens, Jugtown's current owner, made this decorated canister set.

JUGTOWN'S FUTURE A FAMILY
AFFAIR: James H. Owen, whose family
includes many potters, like his nephew,
Charlie Owen, (1901-1992) seen here,
produced some of Jugtown Pottery's first
wares. Today, Jim Owen's grandson, Vernon
(1941-), seen here at the wheel in 1974,
and his wife, former Jugtown apprentice,
Pamela Lorette Owens, own and operate
the pottery. Their son, Travis, daughter,
Bayle, and Vernon's brother, Bobby (1939-),
keep Jugtown's traditions alive. *Charlie Owen
photo courtesy of Ben Owen III.*

DONNA CRAVEN POTTERY: Donna Craven's small stature belies her ability to turn large vessels like this piece emerging from the yawning mouth of her wood-burning kiln. Her coiled and wheel-turned wares may bear signs of her trademark taping technique, whereas the addition of manganese, crackle slips, and ash glaze creates beautifully decorated wares like this lidded jar. The Craven family has been associated with North Carolina pottery-making since the earliest years of Seagrove area settlement. *Photos courtesy of Donna Craven.*

DOVER POTTERY: Established in 1983 by Al and Milly McCanless, Dover Pottery was the fourteenth shop to open in Seagrove's "new era" of pottery production. Milly McCanless stands at the entry to Dover's rustic sales shop, where inside, visitors find beautifully decorated crystalline-glazed porcelain, like the blue crystal-encrusted vase shown here, and hand-painted majolica wares displayed in ancient cupboards and on weathered table-tops. Today, Al and Milly's sons, Will and Eck, operate their own potteries nearby.

POTTERS BEGET POTTERS:
Jim Owen's son, Melvin Lee (1917-2003), long a journeyman potter laboring in many Seagrove area shops, established his own pottery on the site where his father once turned his wares. This tattered photo shows some of M. L.'s children, all future pottery workers, including Ina, Boyd, Lula Belle, Vernon, and Viola. Their mother, Marie Garner Owens (1919-1988), shown here glazing wares for the family shop, was no stranger to the trade herself. M. L. added the *s* to the Owens family name. *Photos courtesy of Boyd Owens.*

WORK WHERE THERE'S WORK
TO DO: It was common for potters
like Jonah Owen (1895-1966),
one of four brothers who made
pottery (Jonah, Walter, Melvin,
and Elvin), to find work away from
the family shop. The "sine wave"
decorated jar on the left was most
likely made by J. H. Owen, and
the black-glazed example on the
right was probably made by his
son, Jonah, for Lee County's North
State Pottery Company. It bears the
pottery's earliest stamped mark.
Jonah Owen is seen here standing at
the pottery's traditional treadle wheel.
Jonah Owen photograph courtesy of
The State Archives of North Carolina.

45

ECK MCCANLESS POTTERY:
Eck McCanless often spends the
first hours in his shop each day
playing guitar before moving to
the wheel to create his distinctive
line of carved agateware. As many
as four colors of clay are turned
together before being carved
to reveal fascinating designs.
Agateware is an ancient type of
pottery, and centuries ago it was
a mainstay of some of England's
finest Staffordshire potters. In
addition to agateware, Eck creates
crystalline pottery for sale in his
family's nearby Dover Pottery.
Photos courtesy of Eck McCanless.

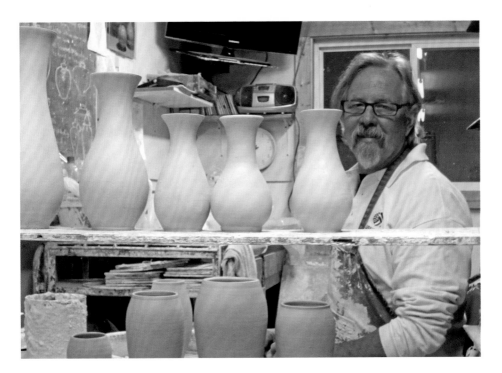

FRANK NEEF POTTERY: Seagrove newcomers, Frank Neef and his wife Cindy, set up shop in the historic Auman house in downtown Seagrove in 2010. Frank began making pottery in 1975, followed by a stint as a production potter in Branson, Missouri. Influenced by Chinese and Korean porcelain masters, and art nouveau potter Adelaide Robineau, he creates crystalline-glazed wares and intricately pierced vessels requiring many hours of painstaking work. *Photos courtesy of Frank Neef.*

COOPERS' NORTH STATE POTTERY:
Following the success of the Busbee's
Jugtown Pottery, Lee County residents
Henry (1886-1959) and Rebecca Palmer
(1886-1954) Cooper, seen here outside their
log sales shop, started North State Pottery
near Sanford, in the 1920s. This North
State stoneware vase features a crackle and
red reduction glaze. Potters working for
North State Pottery included Jonah Owen,
Charlie Craven, and Walter N. Owen. *Cooper
photo courtesy of North Carolina Collection, The
University of North Carolina at Chapel Hill Library.*

CHARLIE CRAVEN FILLED NORTH STATE ROLE: Charlie Boyd Craven (1909-1991) was denied the opportunity to work for Jugtown Pottery by his father, potter Daniel Craven, who said that his labor was needed at home. In time, the Coopers employed him at North State Pottery. A young Charlie Craven, who could turn up to sixty pounds of clay, is seen standing at North State's treadle wheel and during a well deserved break. *Photos courtesy of The State Archives of North Carolina, and North Carolina Collection, The University of North Carolina at Chapel Hill Library.*

FROM THE GROUND UP POTTERY: Michael Mahan, here with his son, Levi, has been a Seagrove area potter for more than a quarter century. He opened Wild Rose Pottery in the Whynot community before starting From the Ground Up Pottery around 1998. His shop is on the site of an 1890s pottery operated by W. J. Stewart. He makes southwestern and ash-glazed dinnerware, "soul pots," meditation bells, and tree-decorated wares evoking memories of past civilizations' ancient mystical and sacred reverence for trees. *Photos courtesy of Michael Mahan.*

GREAT WHITE OAK GALLERY: Benjamin and Bonnie Burns operate The Great White Oak Gallery in the town of Seagrove where they produce vividly colored wares in glazes including oxblood red, rutile blue, iridescent green, and a white over black combination. Benjamin learned the pottery-making craft at the Ceramic League of Miami before making pottery at Pitter the Potter in Maggie Valley, North Carolina. Bonnie's work includes wheel-turned and hand-built wares and decorated tiles. *Photos courtesy of Benjamin and Bonnie Burns.*

NORTH STATE'S RUSTIC SHOP SETTING: Typical of the area's many historic rural potteries run by farmer-potters, North State Pottery Co.'s 1920s site consisted of a few sheds, like this one protecting two groundhog-type kilns, at the time called, "Chinese pottery kilns," and log pole buildings like this sales shop, here hosted by the owners' daughters, Geneva and Dorothy Susan. Photos *courtesy of North Carolina Collection, University of North Carolina at Chapel Hill Library.*

ROADSIDE SHOPS ESSENTIAL TO POTTERY SALES: Roadside stands mounted along busy roadways like US Route 1 played an important role in promoting sales of remotely made Seagrove-area art pottery. This modest stand features North State Pottery and other crafts. A Sanford shop operated by Neill A. Cole also sold North State Pottery. This amazing postcard view shows pottery perched on porch rails, roofs, and about every inch of flat ground. *Roadside stand photo courtesy of The State Archives of North Carolina. Neill A. Cole postcard, collection of the author.*

HUMBLE MILL POTTERY: In the 1970s, Jerry Fenberg and Charlotte Wooten Fenberg established Humble Mill Pottery when few Seagrove-area potteries were in operation. Trained at the Memphis Academy of Art, they were sponsored in Japan by potter, Shoji Hamada. They were influenced by nearby potters including members of the Auman, Owen, Cole, and Teague families. Following Jerry's death, Charlotte continues to hand paint Humble Mill wares made by Kurt Brantner and Patrick Lowe. *Photos courtesy of Charlotte Wooten Fenberg.*

JLK Jewelry at Jugtown Pottery: JLK Jewelry is an enterprise of Jennie Lorette Keatts. Jennie creates beautiful jewelry from silver, gold, and copper. A hallmark of her craft is the use of cabochons made of glazed pottery. Each piece is handmade, and the glazes for Jennie's "pottery gemstones" are developed by her sister, Pamela Lorette Owens, co-owner of Jugtown Pottery. Seen here with torch in hand, Jennie is preparing the metalwork portion of her jewelry for the attachment of richly glazed cabochons. *Photos courtesy of Jennie Lorette Keatts.*

HANDMADE, OR NOT AT ALL: North State Pottery's owner, Henry Cooper, here at the wheel, learned enough about the art to show shop visitors how every piece of pottery was handmade. Jason B. Cole (1869-1943) displays a vase made by him at his J. B. Cole's Pottery, where for decades, his son, daughter, and two sons-in-law created beautiful art wares. *Cooper photo courtesy of The State Archives of North Carolina. Cole photo courtesy of North Carolina Collection, The University of North Carolina at Chapel Hill Library. Bayard Wootten photo.*

OLD WAYS, NEW IDEAS: A diminished demand for utilitarian wares led some potters to abandon their trade, while others used their knowledge of clay, glaze, and fire to create "art pottery." Except for unusual folds of clay at its neck, and cobalt blue color, this transitional lead-glazed earthenware jar, hand signed by J. B. Cole, looks a lot like a churn. Seen here about 1933-36, Cole initially used a traditional groundhog kiln to finish his pottery. *Kiln photo courtesy of Pack Memorial Library North Carolina Collection. Jackson C. Felmet photo.*

JOHNSTON AND GENTITHES
STUDIOS: Alfred University College of
Ceramics graduates, Fred Johnston and
Carol Gentithes, occupy a site near the
center of the town of Seagrove. Curious
and creative, both like to experiment.
They excel in finding new ways to
express themselves with clay, glaze, and
fire. Often awarded for their work, they
have been highlighted in numerous
exhibitions and publications. Carol
sculpts a rhinoceros while Fred stands in
the opening of their monumental wood-
fired kiln. *Photos courtesy of Fred Johnston
and Carol Gentithes.*

JOSEPH SAND POTTERY: A
Minnesotan by birth, Joseph
Sand came to North Carolina
to complete an apprenticeship
with potter Mark Hewitt. He
decided to become a potter while
studying at England's University
of Wolverhampton. Since 2009,
he has operated his own pottery
near Randleman, North Carolina,
where he makes functional and
sculptural pottery. Construction of
his enormous kiln, seen here, was
enabled in part by a grant from
the Ella Fountain Pratt Emerging
Artist Award program. *Photos
courtesy of Joseph Sand.*

A FAMILY AFFAIR: Much like farming, traditional pottery-making in the Seagrove area was an everyday, family affair. Bill Cole, the son of potter Waymon Cole (1905-1987), plays in a pot in front of his grandfather's J. B. Cole's Pottery shop. Bill Cole attentively looks on as his father pierces holes in clay to make cut flower vases. *Shop photo courtesy of the North Carolina Folklife Institute. Waymon Cole photo courtesy of North Carolina Collection, The University of North Carolina at Chapel Hill Library. Bayard Wootten photo.*

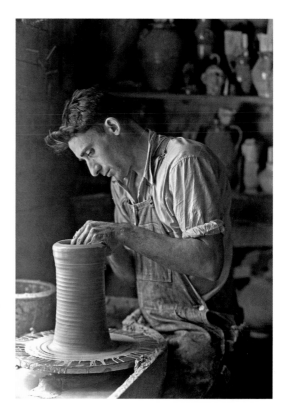

A MASTER AT THE WHEEL:
Potter Waymon Cole was a true master of
the art and mystery of pottery-making.
From modestly-sized forms, to impressively
large floor vases like the one seen here,
Waymon Cole's work is prized today by
collectors and museums alike. *Waymon
Cole photo courtesy of North Carolina
Collection, The University of North Carolina at
Chapel Hill Library. Bayard Wootten photo.*

JUGTOWN POTTERY: Established in the 1920s by Jacques and Juliana Busbee, Jugtown Pottery is owned today by Vernon and Pamela Lorette Owens. Vernon is a North Carolina Folk Heritage Award recipient and Jugtown Pottery is listed in the National Register of Historic Places. Pam first came to Jugtown as an apprentice potter. The Owens's son, Travis, is seen here creating a large wheel-turned vessel. In this photograph, examples of Jugtown pottery are shown featuring the work of (L-R) Vernon, Travis, and Pamela Owens.

KING'S POTTERY: Lifelong Seagrove residents, Terry and Anna King, first learned the pottery trade with the late Walter and Dorothy Cole Auman, owners of Seagrove Pottery. Their first shop opened at the site of the old Joe Owen Pottery on highway 705 in 1987. Anna was also mentored by local potter, Charlie Owen. The Kings are known for their expressive face jugs as well as other sculptural creations and functional wares. Their daughter, Crystal King, operates her own shop near Seagrove. *Photos courtesy of Terry and Anna King.*

CONTRACT WORK ENSURED SUCCESS: Much of the success realized by Seagrove's first art potteries resulted from contracts made to produce wares for sale at gift shops, tourist resorts, and department stores. Bascome King (1895-1952), son-in-law of J. B. Cole, seen here at the wheel, made many of the vases marked Sunset Mountain Pottery. Both handled vases seen here bear this mark, and were made around 1930 for sale in Asheville. *King photo courtesy of Randolph Room, Historical Photograph Collection, Randolph County Public Library.*

AN ENDLESS TASK: From ground to wheel, clay goes through many steps of preparation, including a process called pugging, being accomplished here by Herman Cole (1895-1982). Clay is mixed and extruded into uniform shapes before being cut into manageable sections. Once on the wheel, it's the potter's task to apply strength and skill to the clay to create vessels like these made by Philmore Graves (1904-1969). *Photos courtesy of the North Carolina Folklife Institute and The State Archives of North Carolina.*

LIBERTY STONEWARE:
Sited some distance from
Seagrove near Snow Camp,
North Carolina, Brenda
Hornsby Heindl's shop fits
well into the Seagrove pottery
scene. Utilizing local clays and
a newly constructed wood-
fired kiln, Brenda specializes
in salt-glazed stoneware. A
student of historic American
pottery production, she
completed Berea College's
Ceramics Apprenticeship
Program and the Winterthur
Program in American Material
Culture. *Photos courtesy of
Brenda Hornsby Heindl. Kiln photo
by Oliver Mueller-Heubach.*

LUCK'S WARE POTTERY: Sid Luck traces his pottery-making ancestry back four generations to William Luck (b. *c.* 1811), whose daughter, Sarah Jane, married potter Evan Cole. Formerly a Marine, and then a chemistry teacher, Sid returned to his pottery roots when he opened Luck's Ware Pottery in 1987. Still a teacher at heart, Sid mentors Seagrove elementary school kids in the art of pottery making through the North Carolina Pottery Center's educational programs. *Photos courtesy of Sid Luck. Ben Albright photos.*

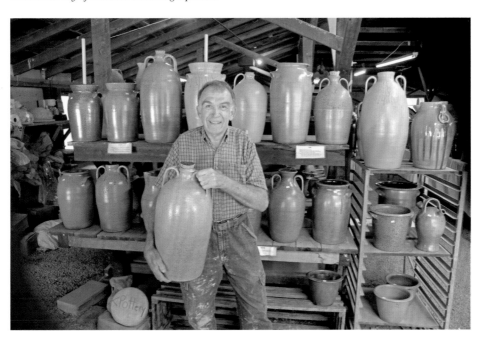

WOMEN ESSENTIAL TO ART POTTERY SUCCESS: Women like Nell Cole Graves (1908-1997) were instrumental to the success of many early Seagrove area art potteries. Her wares are known for thinly turned walls and refined shapes. She stood toe-to-toe in ability with her brother, Waymon Cole, her husband, Philmore Graves, and brother-in-law, Bascome King, who for decades produced art wares for her father's J. B. Cole's Pottery. *Bayard Wootten photos courtesy of North Carolina Collection, The University of North Carolina at Chapel Hill Library.*

MANY BRANCHES ON COLE POTTERY
TREE: Evan Cole's son, Ruffin Cole
(1859-1931), seen here with his wife, Ella
Trogdon, initially turned for his brother
Franklin Cole. Evan Cole's seven pottery-
making sons left an indelible mark on
North Carolina's success as a center for
pottery production. Ruffin's son, Arthur
Ray Cole (1892-1974), seen here with his
wife, Pauline Cox, joined three brothers,
Charles C. (1887-1967), Everette (1897-
1974), and Clarence (1906-1937), in the
making of another generation of potters.
Photos courtesy of Neolia Cole.

MCCANLESS POTTERY: The son of Dover Pottery founders, Al and Milly McCanless, Peder Wilhelm (Will) McCanless opened his own shop in 2006. Located a few miles from Seagrove on highway 705, his shop offers delicately decorated hand painted stoneware, like the exquisite example seen here, along with wares coated in Seagrove Red, and zinc silicate crystalline glazes. Will has traveled to China, Malaysia, France, Italy, and Great Britain to study the world's ceramic traditions. *Photos courtesy of Will McCanless.*

MICHÈLE HASTINGS AND JEFF BROWN POTTERY: Michèle Hastings first met Jeff Brown when she was his student in a pottery class at the New Hampshire Institute of Art. Jeff was an instructor there from 2002-2009 following a period in the 1980s and 1990s when he worked as a journeyman potter in and out of the Seagrove area. Now, together, these self-proclaimed "Gypsy Potters" produce functional and decorative vessels in their shop located on the outskirts of Seagrove in the Whynot community. *Photos courtesy of Michèle Hastings and Jeff Brown.*

RAINBOW POTTERY DRAWS
SEAGROVE TO SANFORD: Arthur
Ray Cole opened his own pottery
near Seagrove in 1927. Then, about
1934, he relocated to Sanford, in Lee
County, where he turned for Maurice
Sylvester Leverett's (1972-1943) Rainbow
Pottery Company. Here, he is seen in
the original log shop with Leverett's
daughter, Marguerite. Leverett sold
Rainbow Pottery Company to Cole, and
the operation was renamed A. R. Cole
Pottery. A page from a Rainbow Pottery
catalog is seen here displaying some
shapes made by A. R. Cole. *Photos courtesy
of Neolia Cole.*

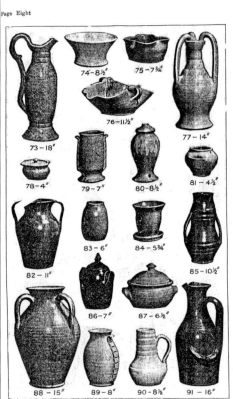

PRICE LIST AND DESCRIPTION

No. 73 Roman Pitcher, reproduced from a design popular in the ancient Roman Empire. Price $2.50

No. 74 Connecticut Bowl. Perfect for a loose arrangement of flowers. Price 90c

No. 75 The Clover-Leaf. This unique bowl presents its loveliest picture when filled with a mass of small, short stemmed flowers. Price 90c

No. 76 Fruit Bowl of uncommon shape. Price $1.75

No. 77 Assyrian Vase. Found in the excavation of the tomb of a princess in old Assyria. The pottery was thought to have been of Egyptian origin, since the tomb had been sealed for 5,000 years. Large size $2.50; small size $1.50

No. 78 Onion soup bowl. Price 50c

No. 79 A very popular flower vase. Price $1.25

No. 80 The pretty simplicity of this lamp-base makes it adaptable to lamp shades of unusual patterns. Price $1.25

No. 81 Swinging Basket, or Ivy Jar. Price 65c

No. 82 Pinehurst Vase. A symmetrical and handsome ornament, and an imposing receptacle for dahlias, chrysanthemums and similar flowers. Price $1.75

No. 83 A little number that is smart in its absurd simplicity. Price 70c

No. 84 Flower pot with attached saucer. Price 85c

No. 85 Graceful vase with strap handles adaptable for flowers or a lamp base. Price $1.50

No. 86 Old-fashioned Ginger Jar. Price $1.50

No. 87 Casserole. Tempered for oven heat. Price $1.50

No. 88 A vase that combines dignity with beauty, in a style suggestive of the Grecian Amphora. Price $3.50

No. 89 A vase whose novel lines appeal to seekers of the unusual. Price $1.50

No. 90 Pueblo Pitcher, often used as a vase. Price $1.25

No. 91 Rebecca Pitcher, from the Biblical design. Price $3.00

STRATEGIC LOCATION PERFECT FOR SALES: A young Neolia Cole, daughter of Arthur Ray Cole, sits on, and stands by the porch of the original Rainbow Pottery Company sales shop, which after the pottery's purchase by her father became A. R. Cole Pottery. The shop's signs and pottery examples beckoned to U. S. highway 1 travelers, suggesting that they, "Stop—See It Made—Hand-Made." Following the shop's closure due to highway construction, the operation was relocated a few miles away on US Highway 15-501. *Photos courtesy of Neolia Cole.*

NEW SALEM POTTERY: New Salem Pottery is named for northern Randolph County's historic New Salem Quaker village. Nearby is the site of a late eighteenth- to early nineteenth-century earthenware pottery operated by Quaker William Dennis. Hal E. and Eleanor Minnock-Pugh dig clay from their land to create examples of beautifully slip-trailed decorated earthenware. Eleanor places delicate lines of slip onto an engobe-coated dish before firing it in a kiln. *Pottery photo courtesy of Hal E. Pugh and Eleanor Minnock-Pugh.*

OLD GAP POTTERY: Open since 1972, Phillip Pollet's Old Gap Pottery is one of Seagrove's oldest "new era" shops. Phil's work is a fusion of Asian and Western influences. Often asymmetrical in shape, his pieces are sometimes hand-altered, carved, stamped, and hand painted creating fine examples of stoneware, earthenware, porcelain, and Raku pottery. Here, Phil is stamp decorating a wheel thrown and hand-altered vase. In this image, he is placing a pot into a Raku drop kiln preheated to 2,000° F. *Photos courtesy of Phillip Pollet.*

SATURDAY MORNING FREE-FOR-ALL:
The demand for examples of A. R. Cole pottery,
like the large multi-colored floor vase seen
here, once brought crowds of people and a
free-for-all atmosphere to the old shop on
Saturday mornings following Cole's emptying of
his latest kiln-load of wares. This shop building
was constructed in Sanford's North View
community following the pottery's relocation
in the 1970s. *Shop photo courtesy of Neolia Cole.*

ANOTHER COLE TAKES SEAGROVE TO SMITHFIELD: Good river clay and a concrete highway heavily traveled by northern tourists drew Herman Cole to Johnston County in 1927 to establish Smithfield Art Pottery, first called Hillside Pottery. He employed some of the region's best potters, including journeymen from Georgia and Texas. This flambé-glazed jar is typical of Smithfield's superb quality. Construction of huge bottle kilns like this one may have contributed to the closure of this pottery around 1942. *Kiln photo courtesy of the North Carolina Folklife Institute.*

ORIGINAL OWENS POTTERY:

On the spot where their grandfather, James H. Owen, and father, Melvin Lee Owens, made pottery for many decades, Boyd Owens and his sister, Nancy Owens Brewer, continue to operate Original Owens Pottery. Perhaps best known today for their vivid red glaze, this shop specializes in functional tablewares and decorative items for home use. Here, Nancy Owens Brewer works at the wheel while another load of red pottery emerges from a successful kiln burn. *Photos courtesy of Boyd Owens.*

PHIL MORGAN POTTERY: Phil Morgan has been making pottery at his shop near the heart of Seagrove since its opening in 1973. Perhaps best known for his outstanding crystalline-glazed wares, Phil, his wife Julia, and son and daughter-in-law, produce utilitarian wares in other glazes as well. Here, Phil is joined by helpers and friends in burning another successful load of pottery, resulting in wares like these dazzling crystalline-glazed porcelain vases. *Photos courtesy of Phil Morgan. Ben Albright photos.*

ROYAL CROWN POTTERY AND PORCELAIN COMPANY: Opened in 1939 by Russian immigrant, and New York silver shop owner, Victor Obler (1894-1974), Royal Crown Pottery produced high-quality art pottery until 1942. Located away from Seagrove in Chatham County's Merry Oaks community, the shop employed Moore and Randolph County potters, including Charlie Craven, who had worked for North State Pottery and Smithfield Art Pottery. Much of Royal Crown's output was sold in New York. *Shop photo courtesy of The State Archives of North Carolina.*

CAROLINA CRAFT POTTERY:
Brothers Everette Cole (1897-1974)
and Charles C. Cole (1887-1967)
operated Carolina Craft Pottery
near New Hill in Wake County
from about 1927-1933. Everette
Cole is seated to the right of his
brother, Arthur Ray Cole. Aided
by R. Emmitt Albright (1910-1996),
Carolina Craft produced salt-glazed
stoneware and earthenware art
pottery. Marked examples may
bear a paper label or an impressed
stamped mark reading, CAROLINA
CRAFT/AMERICAN/HANDMADE.
Cole photo courtesy of Neolia Cole.

ROCK HOUSE POTTERY: Established by Kenneth and Carolyn Kennedy Poole in 1983, Rock House Pottery specializes in pottery with hand carved surfaces including dogwood blossoms, pine cones, dragonflies, oak leaves, tulips, and grape clusters. Carolyn springs from a line of traditional potters including William Davis whose log pottery shop was located at Westmoore just a short distance away from Rock House Pottery.

SEAGROVE STONEWARE: With their gallery located in Seagrove's original general store, and with their Victorian bed and breakfast inn next door, Alexa Modderno and David Fernandez, although relatively new to the region, have established their Seagrove Stoneware shop in the very heart of historic Seagrove. In their own individual styles, Alexa and David create a variety of functional and decorative pottery coated in custom-made, vibrantly colored glazes. *Photos courtesy of David Fernandez and Alexa Modderno.*

C. C. COLE POTTERY:

A copperhead bite to his hand limited his work as a potter, yet Charlie Cole (1887-1967) operated a successful Moore County shop after purchasing the site from James G. Teague (1906-1988). In 1939, Teague moved to New Jersey to make pottery for J. M. Stangl. Up to 3,000 items a day were made by Thurston, Dorothy, and Everette Cole, and Virginia King Shelton. Charlie Cole stands in front of a full kiln. The two pottery examples are attributed to Thurston Cole. *Kiln photo courtesy of the North Carolina Folklife Institute.*

SEAGROVE POTTERY a COLE-AUMAN CONNECTION:

Begun first as an outlet for her father's C. C. Cole Pottery, Seagrove Pottery was established by Dorothy Cole (b. 1925), and her husband, Walter Auman (b. 1926), whose family ran another important Seagrove area pottery. For many years, Seagrove Pottery was a must-see stop when visiting the region's potteries. In 1991, Dorothy and Walter Auman were killed in an automobile accident involving a logging truck. *Photos courtesy of Randolph Room, Historical Photograph Collection, Randolph County Public Library.*

STUEMPFLE POTTERY:

Pennsylvanian David Stuempfle set up his own Seagrove pottery following a stint as a student of Isobel Karl at New Hampshire's High Mowing School, and apprenticeships in Tennessee, and at Jugtown Pottery. His original 1992 kiln is a thirty-foot long cross-draft monster requiring up to 150 hours to fire. More recently, Estonian kiln-builder Andres Allik, helped build a new anagama kiln. The natural confluence of clay, wood ash, and fire produces Stuempfle stoneware masterpieces. *Photos courtesy of David Stuempfle.*

TURN AND BURN POTTERY: David and Deborah Garner have spent twenty years making pottery in Seagrove, but are best known by many people as demonstration potters at the NC State Fair's Village of Yesteryear. Raku-type pottery; salt-glazed, wood-fired stoneware; and wares with horsehair-decorated surfaces make up much of Turn and Burn's production. David's ancestors made pottery nearby, and besides being a potter, he once served as Seagrove's mayor and is a church pastor today. *Kiln photo courtesy of David and Deborah Garner.*

POTTERY HERITAGE TIED TO COMMUNITY AND FAMILIES: Potters Dorothy and Walter Auman were keenly aware of their community's importance as a unique center of pottery production. They opened the Seagrove Pottery Museum in a relocated Seagrove train depot, filling it with their own collection of historic pottery. Much of their collection, with examples similar to these made at Seagrove's Auman Pottery, is now in the collection of Charlotte's Mint Museum. *Museum photo courtesy of Randolph Room, Historical Photograph Collection, Randolph County Public Library.*

TEAGUE POTTERY SITE A CLASSIC
EXAMPLE: Bryan D. "Duck" Teague's
(1898-1983) shop, opened about
1929, included a log workroom, a
mule-drawn pug mill for mixing clay,
and a semi-subterranean groundhog
kiln. Pottery topped one structure, with
a sign reading: TEAGUE POTTERY/STOP/
SEE IT MADE. Daughter Zedith Teague
Garner (1927-1976) prepares pottery
for sale in 1975. *Site photo courtesy of the
North Carolina Folklife Institute. Zedith Teague
photo courtesy of Pack Memorial Library North
Carolina Collection. Jan Schochet photo.*

UWHARRIE CRYSTALLINE POTTERY:
Named for a nearby ancient mountain range,
Uwharrie Crystalline Pottery is operated by
William and Pamela Kennedy, seen here working
side by side at their own wheels. With little
formal training, the Kennedy's have mastered
the painstaking process of making crystals
appear in their beautifully colored glazes.
The addition of cobalt, copper, and nickel to
the crystal-growing zinc oxide component
of their glaze creates a wide range of colors.
Photos courtesy of William and Pamela Kennedy.

W. M. HEWITT POTTERY:

Although his shop is located away from Seagrove in Chatham County, Mark Hewitt's influence on the Seagrove pottery scene is clearly seen in the work of nearby former apprentices like Daniel Johnston and Joseph Sand. Here, Mark is seen working on one of his monumental vessels, with apprentices Joseph Sand and Alex Matisse in the background. Mark was born in Stone, Staffordshire, England, and apprenticed to potter Michael Cardew before coming to the US. *Photos courtesy of Mark Hewitt.*

OLD PLANK ROAD POTTERY:
In 1959, Ben Owen Sr. opened a pottery at Westmoore called Old Plank Road Pottery. It was at this point in his career that Ben Owen, after thirty-seven years as Jugtown's potter, claimed the title "Master Potter." Ben Owen was assisted by potter Lester Farrell Craven (1911-1972), his son Benjamin Wade Owen Jr. (1937-2002), his grandson, Ben Owen III (1968-), Boyce Yow (1902-1986) and others. Here, Ben Owen is creating one of his signature tall candlesticks. *Photos courtesy of The State Archives of North Carolina.*

ALWAYS SOMETHING TO DO: Pottery is air-dried before being glazed and burned at temperatures sometimes exceeding 2,000° F. Some products require a first run through the kiln without glaze, called a bisque firing, followed by one or more additional firings, including a final glaze, or glost, firing. Here, Boyce Yow and Wade Owen prepare Old Plank Road wares for finishing. They are most likely marked BEN OWEN/MASTER POTTER. *Boyce Yow photo courtesy of The State Archives of North Carolina. Wade Owen photo courtesy of Ben Owen III.*

WESTMOORE POTTERY:

Started in 1977 by David and Mary Farrell, Westmoore Pottery produces historically inspired stoneware and redware pottery reflecting styles made by North Carolina's earliest potters. Westmoore pottery is found in museums and historic buildings where it is used in period displays. It is not unusual to spot it in historically-based movies. The Westmoore pottery seen here was displayed at Fort Dobbs, an eighteenth-century historic site located in Iredell County. *Photos courtesy of Mary and David Farrell.*

WHYNOT POTTERY AND ACACIA ART TILE: The story goes that the community name, *Whynot*, was chosen by consternated leaders who couldn't agree about a name for a rural post office site. The unique appellation was selected for their pottery name when Mark and Meredith Heywood opened their shop in 1982. The Heywoods say, "We just make pots." But this modest claim misrepresents their exceptional creations including vases, lamps, candlesticks, and tablewares for everyday use. *Photos courtesy of Meredith and Mark Heywood.*

ACKNOWLEDGMENTS

I am indebted to the many potters who generously provided historical and contemporary images for *Seagrove Potteries Through Time*. Likewise, I am thankful for family members of past potters who allowed me access to their treasured ancestors' photographs. In addition, I wish to thank staff representing numerous institutional collections for their assistance in locating and acquiring important historical images for inclusion in this volume. I am truly grateful to Charles G. "Terry" Zug III, the guru of North Carolina pottery studies, who once said to me, "Perhaps you should do a book of photographs." Well, here it is. Finally, I express my appreciation and love to Kathy, who so liberally tolerates my time-consuming passion for North Carolina pottery.

SMITHFIELD ART POTTERY (1927-1942): For a collector of historic North Carolina art pottery, this is what a good dream looks like. Owner Herman Cole and members of his crew stand amid a sea of market-ready pottery. Smithfield potters included Charlie Craven, Farrell Craven, Charlie Teague, Jack Kiser, Bill Gordy, and Guy Daugherty. Cole is quoted as saying, "I don't care how much you make, how many pieces you make. I don't care how much money you make. But every piece has got to be right." *Photo courtesy of the North Carolina Folklife Institute.*